the official guide to
Ballroom Dancing

the official guide to
Ballroom Dancing

Allen Dow
with Mike Michaelson

 **DOMUS BOOKS**
NORTHBROOK, ILLINOIS

Book design and production: Mary MacDonald
Photography: Patrick K. Snook
Type composition: Hagle
Production coordinator: Ruth Guest

THE OFFICIAL GUIDE TO BALLROOM DANCING
Copyright © 1980 Quality Books, Inc.
A Domus Book
Published by
Quality Books, Inc.
400 Anthony Trail
Northbrook, Illinois 60062 U.S.A.

1 2 3 4 5 6 7 8 9 10

Manufactured in the United States of America

Library of Congress Cataloging in Publication Data

Dow, Allen, 1931–
    The official guide to ballroom dancing.

    1. Ballroom dancing.   I. Michaelson, Mike, 1934– joint author
II. Title
GV175.D68   793.3'3   79–55239
ISBN 0–89196–065–1

Contents

Introduction

As the decade of the eighties dawned, the world of dance was giving every indication of turning full circle. Disco dancing, the rage of the previous decade was beginning to lose some of its glitter as a chic and fashionable form of dancing—by no means disappearing, but beginning to find its permanent, less-prominent place in the scheme of things. And ballroom dancing, which had enjoyed its glittering hey-day in the thirties and forties, was beginning to experience a renaissance, as big bands once more were attracting large crowds to dance extravaganzas and dance studios were receiving ever-increasing requests from students for instruction in ballroom techniques.

In its hey-day, ballroom dancing was the biggest game in town, a Saturday-night outing that also was a source of romantic adventure for millions. Dance emporia such as the famous Roseland Dance City in New York—billed as the world's largest dancehall—Chicago's huge Aragon Ballroom and London's Hammersmith Palais de Danse attracted thousands of patrons to dance and listen to such bands as Benny Goodman, the Dorseys, Carmen Cavallaro, Guy Lombardo and Wayne King "The Waltz King." The famous Trocadero Ballroom at the Elitch Gardens in Denver, Colorado, advertised as the summer home of America's big bands, attracted 3,000 dancers on a busy night during the 1930s and kept its doors open until 1976.

Whether ballroom dancing and big bands will return to the dance scene to the extent of their former glory is a matter of conjecture. But without question, ballroom and the big bands are enjoying a rebirth. Undoubtedly, during the eighties, the fox trot, rumba, waltz and tango will take their place alongside the hustle!

CHAPTER 1

Ballroom Basics

Each of the following chapters of this book present instruction for a wide repertoire of ballroom dances, from waltz, fox trot and polka to swing and Latin. Detailed, step-by-step descriptions and corresponding photographs provide easy-to-follow instructions for both the man's and woman's steps. However, before you begin to tackle the basics of these dances, be sure to study the pointers on style, technique and rhythm contained in this chapter.

BASIC STYLING, CLOSED POSITION (American and European Dances)

For the waltz, fox trot and polka, basic styling has the man's *lead arm* (right arm) around partner with hand placed close to the small of her back and elbow parallel to the floor (do not allow elbow to droop). The woman's left elbow is approximately on the man's right elbow, her left hand falling where it may on man's right shoulder.

The *style arm* (his left, her right) has hands palm-to-palm, with fingers and thumbs relaxed around each others hands, fingers between partner's index finger and thumb. An exception is American swing, where positioning of style hand usually

STYLE ARM POSITIONS (Ballroom)

STYLE ARM POSITIONS (Swing)

has man's thumb on top of partner's hand (her hand palm down). In this case, his hand is wrapped outside of woman's hand (little-finger side) with his fingers on her palm.

In *closed position,* feet should be together to begin a dance. Shoulders should be squared off to each other and the woman should be looking at her partner or over her left hand (which rests on his right shoulder). While executing steps for waltz and fox trot, dancers should endeavor to keep knees relaxed and avoid bouncing and swaying. The object is to achieve a smooth, flowing look and feeling. To this end, dancers also should use, in these two dances, long, gliding steps, leading with the ball of the foot.

CLOSED POSITION
(American & European dances)

In swing, excessive bouncing also should be avoided, but some swaying motion is in order. Polka is a fun, lively dance in which bouncy motions are permitted and can contribute to the mood and in which some swaying motion is desirable on the *chassé (see separate definition).*

BASIC STYLING, CLOSED POSITION (Latin Dances)

In the Latin dances, rumba, mambo and cha-cha, the man's lead arm (hand on partner's back) should be *above* the small of the back proportionate to the partner's relative height. Therefore, the man's lead arm (his right) has the elbow slightly higher than in the waltz and other dances previously discussed. His style arm also is equally elevated during these three Latin dances. (Refer to the *Latin motion* section of the rumba chapter for a description of movements during steps of these three dances.)

Tango styling features contra-body motion in addition to long steps with bent (this means *more* than flexed) knees—elements which are imperative for the correct look and feeling of this dance. Styling is more fully described in the tango chapter.

Samba also has a unique styling, characterized by a leaning forward and back

CLOSED POSITION (Latin dances)

motion and by a "barrel-roll" effect with partners in a close closed position. (Again, more explicit styling instructions are included in the samba chapter.)

Merengue has a distinctive leg motion—a kind of "limp" step—initiated by the rib cage and hips. (See merengue chapter for an in-depth discussion of styling and the interesting story of the supposed origin of this dance.)

DEFINITIONS

Supporting leg. Leg holding body weight.

Working leg. Leg in motion.

Steps. A step simply is a change of weight; shifting weight from one foot to the other. Forward, back, side and diagonal steps are taken relative to the direction of the hips. An in-place step is one in which the foot leaves the floor and returns to its original placement (although, not in all cases returning to face the same direction).

Rhythms and timing. The term "rhythm" as used throughout this book is defined as the number of beats of music per step. Timing is the dancer's ability to coordinate his or her rhythm to the rhythm of the music.

As defined in this book, a slow step is one step to two beats of music; dancer would step on count 1, count 2 either a hold or *follow through* (see separate definition). A quick step is one step per beat; dancer would step on each beat of music. For a split step, a dancer would take two steps to one beat of music. Slow, quick or split rhythms (as opposed to steps) refer to dance elements that do not have changes of weight, such as a balance in the waltz where dancers balance on count 2 (second quick) and hold count 3 (third quick).

Chassé. Chassé rhythm is comprised of one quick and one split, count 1-and-2. In chassé steps, one foot "chases" rather than passes the other, as chassé forward right, left foot forward but *not* catching or passing right, right foot forward. Chassés may be executed in any direction.

Turns. Turning is done with movement rather than steps, i.e., a turn is initiated from the upper torso—usually preceding the step on which the turn occurs—and in a constant, flowing motion rather than sporadically, allowing feet to turn on forward and back motions.

Twinkle. This is an element of dance upon which many steps are built (see waltz and fox trot chapters for examples). A twinkle is a change of direction and a change of weight with the feet together. The change of direction is initiated with a *pivot* (a turn, initiated by the upper torso, involving swiveling on the ball of the foot) usually a ¼ or ½ turn.

Follow through. This is a motion allowing continuity and direction from one step to another. For example, a *forward follow through* would be one leg passing the other in a forward motion; a *back follow through* would be one leg passing the other in a backward motion; a *diagonal follow through* is to go diagonally from one point to another in a straight line; a *curved follow through* is to go from one point to another, as to describe an arc with the foot.

POSITIONS

Inward follow through. From second position (feet apart, side by side) one foot approaches, but does not reach the other, then again moves to the side from which it began.

Back cross follow through. (As in back step in single time swing.) Feet side to side as described in the inward follow through (above), then follow through foot slides back and lifts off floor, crossing in back of supporting leg.

Drop. (As in left open merengue.) When stepping from one foot to another, knee bends on leg which is about to take the weight (before weight transfer occurs) causing body to suddenly lower according to bend in knee.

Visual lead. (As in cha-cha and mambo.) Partners have no physical contact.

Fan. (As in tango.) While pivoting on ball of foot of supporting leg, working leg moves as if to decribe an arc on floor with inside of foot, heel off floor (turn out position).

The wrap step. (As in swing and rumba.) Working leg wraps around and close to supporting leg on to ball of foot.

Closed position. (See basic styling, beginning of this chapter.)

Left open position. (Also known as "conversation position.") Man's left shoulder open slightly, woman's left shoulder open slightly with man's right arm around her waist and, usually, man's left hand holding her right hand.

Right open position. As above, reversing shoulder motion.

Right side position. Man's right upper torso from center to right of woman's upper torso, partners facing each other.

Left side position. Exact opposite of above.

Left parallel position. Partners facing same direction with woman to the right of man (some physical contact, such as man's right hand holding partner's left hand, man's right arm around her waist, etc.).

Right parallel position. Exact opposite of above.

Apart position. No physical contact between partners, as described in chassé in cha-cha and mambo chapters.

Turn out. A term that describes the action of the inside of the heel of the foot pulling forward.

CHAPTER 2

The Waltz

It is difficult to believe that the graceful, elegant waltz once was decried as an "immoral" dance that scandalized 18th century Europe. Yet, in regions of Germany and Switzerland, the dance was outlawed because it involved close body contact between partners that was considered "lewd."

By the early 1800s the waltz had been introduced to a reluctant London society and had crossed the Atlantic to shock religious leaders in the United States. Even as the dance gained acceptance by Americans, it was with the admonishment that the gentleman's hand that came into contact with a lady's waist should be modestly enclosed in a glove, or at least hold a handkerchief to make that daring contact more acceptable. Before long, the waltz was being performed by the cream of New York society at gala affairs, such as the ball held at the Park Theatre to honor Charles Dickens.

But it was Vienna, where the dance was performed at giddy, swirling speed, that became the Waltz Capital of the World. It was here, in the lively taverns of the Vienna Woods, that Josef Lanner and the Strausses first built their international reputations as innovators in this popular dance form.

In this chapter, steps are described for the traditional American waltz and the faster, more classical Viennese waltz.

AMERICAN WALTZ

The American waltz, performed at a much slower tempo than the Viennese waltz, utilizes a basic 1-2-3 count. This dance employs a continuous turning of the body, although, again, this is not as accentuated as it is in the Viennese waltz. Usually, this dance is done in a left turn (as illustrated in the following series of steps), but it may also be done in a right turn.

BASIC BOX STEP

Begin basic from the closed position.

This completes first half of basic. For second half, partners simply reverse roles as follows.

COUNT 1.
Mark forward left, Kim back right.

COUNT 2.
Mark side right, Kim side left.

COUNT 3.
Mark left together right, Kim right together left.

COUNT 1.
Mark back right, Kim forward left.

COUNT 2.
Mark side left, Kim side right.

COUNT 3.
Mark right together left, Kim left together right.

FORWARD AND BACK BALANCE STEP

This is commonly known as the "hesitation" step. It may also be done during turns and is a useful step to get you and your partner out of a traffic jam on the dance floor. Begin in closed position with feet together.

COUNT 1.
Mark forward left, Kim back right.

COUNT 2.
Mark balance right to left, Kim balance left to right.

COUNT 3.
Both partners hold balance position.

COUNT 1.
Mark back right, Kim forward left.

COUNT 2.
Mark balance left to right, Kim balance right to left.

COUNT 3.
Both partners hold balance position.

SIDE BALANCE STEP

Begin in closed position with feet together.

COUNT 1.
Mark side left, Kim side right.

COUNT 2.
Mark balance right to left, Kim balance left to right.

COUNT 3.
Both partners hold balance position.

This completes first half of side balance. Second half of side balance is accomplished simply by partners reversing footwork.

APART BALANCE STEP

Begin in closed position with feet together.

COUNT 1.
Mark forward left, Kim back right.

COUNT 2.
Mark balance right to left, Kim balance left to right. On counts 2, 3 Mark's right hand moves from Kim's back to her side (top of hip).

COUNT 3.
Partners hold balance position.

COUNT 1.
Mark back right, Kim back left. On this count, Mark pushes Kim with both hands, releasing right hand. Arms begin moving up for style.

COUNT 2.
Mark balance left to right, Kim balance right to left. Style arms now extended.

COUNT 3.
Partners hold balance position.

Partners now do last three counts of forward and back balance or, as an alternative, they may wish to move into the last three counts of the basic box step.

COUNT 1.
Mark forward left, Kim forward right. On this count, Mark's right hand is approaching Kim's back, coming into closed position once more.

COUNT 2.
Mark balance right to left, Kim balance left to right. Mark's hand now has returned to Kim's back.

COUNT 3.
Partners hold balance position.

LEFT OPEN BALANCE STEP

Begin in closed position with feet together.

COUNT 1.
Mark forward left, Kim forward right (moving into left open position).

COUNT 2.
Mark balance right to left, Kim balance left to right.

COUNT 3.
Partners hold balance in left open position

COUNT 1.
Mark forward right, Kim forward left. Bodies begin turning back to closed position, causing pivot to occur on Mark's right and Kim's left returning to closed position.

COUNT 2.
Mark side left, Kim side right.

COUNT 3.
Mark right foot together left, Kim left foot together right, returning to closed position.

LEFT OPEN CIRCLE BALANCE STEP

COUNT 1.
From closed position, feet together, Mark steps into left open position, forward left, Kim forward right.

COUNT 2.
Mark balance right to left, Kim balance left to right.

COUNT 3.
Partners hold balance position. On counts 2, 3 the style arms of both partners circle up, into the body, down, away from the body.

COUNT AND.
*Use this half count to begin next sequence. Mark kicks right foot (using a soft snap-kick from the knee down with foot pointed—**not** a kick from the hip.)*

During pivot process, Mark's right heel passes over his left foot. This step usually is followed by the basic box step.

COUNT 1.
Mark crosses right foot in front of left (a tight, or close, cross), Kim steps forward right beginning a partial circle around Mark. During this count Mark pushes Kim back with his right hand and begins pulling style arms to his left. Style arms initiate movement of body to left—not actually pulling, but creating a "pull" look.

COUNT 2.
Mark begins pivoting on balls of both feet, still pushing Kim's back with right hand. Kim steps forward right, continuing partial circle around Mark. (On counts 2, 3 style arms move down into bodies, up and out to closed position styling).

COUNT 3.
Mark drops right heel, right foot taking weight, Kim forward left (still circling), pivoting on left to closed position.

LEFT OPEN TWINKLE STEP

Begin in closed position with feet together.

COUNT 1.
Mark forward left, Kim back right.

COUNT 2.
Mark side right, Kim side left. During this count, Mark raises lead (right) elbow and begins to turn Kim with his right hand on her back into left open position.

COUNT 3.
Mark left together right, Kim right together left.

COUNT 1.
Mark forward right, Kim forward left, both partners turning bodies into closed position, causing a pivot on Mark's right foot, Kim's left foot.

COUNT 2.
Mark side left, Kim side right.

COUNT 3.
Mark right together left, Kim left together right.

VIENNESE WALTZ

Like the American waltz, the Viennese waltz utilizes a basic 1-2-3 count—although, as we have noted, the dance is performed at a much faster tempo. When performing cross steps, one leg should be drawn snugly into the other as turning motion continues. Because of the similarity of these two versions of the waltz, we are providing instructions for only the basic step. For variations, refer to the section on the American waltz and incorporate the various balance steps shown there. The Viennese basic is perhaps more versatile than many other dance basics in that it may be easily reversed into both right and left turns.

VIENNESE BASIC STEP

Begin from closed position. (Note: It is imperative that the body continue a left turning motion throughout the basic.)

COUNT 1.
Allen forward left, Lisa back right. Both turn upper torso left, which initiates a turning motion for the rest of the body.

COUNT 2.
Allen side left, Lisa side right (body continues turning movement).

COUNT 3.
Allen crosses left foot in front of right (on ball of left foot). Lisa brings right foot together left.

This completes the first half of the basic. To complete the basic, dancers simply reverse roles, as follows.

COUNT 1.
Allen back right, Lisa forward left.

COUNT 2.
Allen side right, Lisa side left.

COUNT 3.
Allen brings right together left, Lisa crosses left in front of right on ball of left foot.

CHAPTER 3

Swing

The Lindy Hop, the Shag, the Black Bottom—these are the colorful names of some of the equally colorful dances that ushered in the Age of Swing during the depression years of the early 1930s. This new era supplanted the Age of Jazz, which had dominated the previous decade.

The Age of Swing had its own King—Benny Goodman, who aroused ardent fans as much as any latterday John Travolta—and a large following of frenetic, acrobatic dancers whose antics would make an anything-goes disco of the seventies pale by comparison. Soon, swing became known as "jitterbug" and, as a dance form, it moved partners away from the closed position routines that had been the accepted pattern of ballroom dancing for several centuries. Eventually, swing gave way to the rock dancing of the fifties and sixties, and disco of the seventies.

Today, swing is enjoying a renaissance along with the big bands that dominated the dance scene of the thirties and forties, with the durable Benny Goodman leading the way. Contemporary swing dancing, however, is more structured and subdued with none of the spectacular gymnastics that characterized the frenzied jitterbug of the forties. Nonetheless, swing remains extremely versatile and, because it is so much fun do to, it is one of the most used dances.

There is single-, double- and triple-time swing. Double time lacks luster and seldom is taught or used. Triple-time swing, used for slow-medium tempos, is by far the most popular because it is adaptable to a wide range of music. And if you also add to your dance repertoire single-time swing, which is used for medium-fast tempos (such as an upbeat version of "In The Mood"), you'll find that you can perform swing to just about any music.

For triple-time swing, the dance rhythm is quick-and-split, quick-and-split quick-quick; the count is 1-and-2, 3-and-4, 5, 6. For single-time swing, the rhythm is slow-slow-quick-quick, step on counts 1-3-5-6.

Included in the following instructions are techniques for switching from triple- to single-time swing, and vice versa. (Note: All back steps in swing dancing should be taken on the ball of the foot.)

BASIC 6-COUNT SWING STEP (Triple-Time)

Begin in closed position, feet together. Man's left hand holds woman's right with his thumb on top of her hand, his fingers to her palms.

COUNT 1.
Mark side left, Kim side right.

COUNT AND.
Mark right together left, Kim left together right.

COUNT 2.
Mark side left, Kim side right.

END OF COUNT 2.
Inward follow through. Mark's right foot approaching (but not reaching) his left, Kim's left foot approaching her right.

COUNT 3.
Mark pushing off with left foot stepping side right, Kim pushing off with right foot stepping side left.

COUNT AND.
Mark left together right, Kim right together left.

COUNT 4.
Mark side right, Kim side left.

COUNT 5.
Mark leads Kim into left open position, stepping back left on ball of foot, Kim stepping back right on ball of foot.

COUNT 6.
Mark in place right, pivoting on right into closed position, Kim in place left, pivoting on left into closed position.

Basic may be repeated as many times as desired between other steps.

BASIC 6-COUNT SWING STEP (Single-Time)

Begin in closed position, feet together.

COUNT 1.
Mark side left, Kim side right.

COUNT 2.
Inward follow through.

BASIC 6-COUNT SWING STEP (Single-Time)

COUNT 3.
Mark side right, Kim side left.

COUNT 4.
Back cross follow through. Mark's left foot crosses and lifts behind right leg in sweeping motion, preparing to step down on count 5. Kim's right foot crosses and lifts behind left leg in sweeping motion. During this beat Mark also is beginning to lead Kim into left open position.

COUNT 5.
Mark steps on left foot, still crossing behind right leg, Kim steps on right foot, still crossing behind left leg.

COUNT 6.
Mark in place right, beginning to pivot on right into closed position, Kim in place left, beginning to pivot on left into closed position.

All further swing steps will be shown in single time. To convert single-time steps to triple time, all slow steps (counts 1, 2) become quick-and-split steps (count 1-and-2)— chassé rhythm—stepping in same direction as slow steps as indicated in basic. Side slow steps become side-and-2, forward slow steps become forward-and-2, back slow steps become back-and-2.

6-COUNT WRAP RELEASE (Single-Time)

Start from closed position, feet together. Note: This step has three sets of six counts. It is imperative that man steps on ball of left foot for wrap.

COUNT 1.
Mark side left, Kim side right.

COUNT 2.
Inward follow through.

COUNT 3.
Mark side left, Kim side right.

COUNT 4.
Back cross follow through.

COUNT 5.
Mark wraps left foot around right. Kim in place right. At end of count 5 Mark begins to put pressure on Kim's back; this will cause her to pivot on next count and allow him to unwind his wrap at next count.

COUNT 6.
Mark side right, Kim steps in place left, pivoting on left into open position. Mark still holding Kim's right hand with his left.

6-COUNT WRAP RELEASE (Single-Time)

COUNT 1.
Mark forward left, Kim back right, still in open position.

COUNT 2.
Diagonal follow through.

COUNT 3.
Mark side right, Kim side left.

COUNT 4.
Back cross follow through.

COUNT 5.
Mark back left, Kim back right.

COUNT 6.
Mark in place right, Kim in place left.

COUNT 1.
Mark side left, turning slightly (as if to step around a hula hoop that partner might be standing in). Mark's right arm beginning to come around Kim's waist to closed position. Kim forward right, squaring her body to Mark's (a slight pivot on her right foot may occur to complete closed position).

COUNT 2.
Mark inward follow through, Kim diagonal follow through.

COUNT 3.
Mark side right, Kim side left, partners in closed position.

COUNT 4.
Back cross follow through.

COUNT 5.
*Mark left cross behind right, Kim right cross behind left. NOTE: Do **not** wrap backstep in this or any other step **unless** indicated.*

COUNT 6.
Mark in place right, pivoting on right to closed position, Kim in place left, pivoting on left, returning to closed position.

6-COUNT UNDERARM TUCK (Single-Time)

Begin in closed position, feet together. (Prior to count one, man brings partners' style arms—his left, her right—circling down and in front of bodies, approximately belt high, as he slightly tucks partner's right side of body into him.)

COUNT 1.
Mark in place left, Kim in place right. NOTE: stepping on balls of feet for this count usually helps smooth out step.

COUNT 2.
*Mark takes style arms in downward circle, bringing both partners' arms up over Kim's head, preparing to push her under raised arms with his right hand. End of count 2, Kim pivots on right foot, right shoulder back. (To avoid ducking, all underarm turns actually are done under **hands**, the highest point of the arched arms.)*

COUNT 3.
Mark side right, turning Kim under arm, Kim side left.

COUNT 4.
Follow through.

COUNT 5.
Mark back left, Kim back right. (Remember, back steps are done on balls of feet; note that in open position style arms are extended outward and upward to some degree).

COUNT 6.
Mark in place right, Kim in place left. Kim begins pivot on left foot, left shoulder back, beginning to go under arm.

COUNT 1.
Mark side right, turning Kim under arm. Kim pivots on left foot, left shoulder back, stepping side or, preferably, back on right foot. NOTE: Although illustration shows Kim taking side step with right foot, for a more stylish appearance woman may take a back step instead of a side step, with a little more pivoting on left foot to face partner.

COUNT 2.
Follow through.

COUNT 3.
Mark side right, Kim side left.

COUNT 4.
Back cross follow through.

COUNT 5.
Mark back left, Kim back right.

COUNT 6.
Mark in place right, Kim in place left.

Partners come back together as in last six counts of 6-Count Wrap Release.

CHAPTER 4

Polka

Although often thought of as a Polish-originated dance, the romping polka with its fast, whirling pace and lively hops and stamps actually is Bohemian in origin, the name derived from the Czech *pulka*—half—referring to the half-step used in the dance. In the mid-19th century, the polka swept Paris off its feet—literally and figuratively. By 1848 it was being performed at Buckingham Palace and by 1852 West Point cadets were dancing to the buoyant, beckoning rhythm of the polka.

With this exhilarating beat and movement, polka continues as a perennial favorite and often is called for at least once at spirited social events such as weddings—particularly when the gathering includes people of Eastern European background. This arms-length dance is fun to do and relatively easy to learn—particularly for students who already have mastered the similarities of the samba basic. The steps described and illustrated in this chapter are for a version of the polka that is most universally used in the United States. The version popularly known as the Polish Polka employs a double-hopping motion and is more difficult to master. The following steps use a count of and-1-and-2 (syncopated rhythm). Counts 1-and-2 and 1-and-2 are done in chassé fashion. While doing chassé left, partners should lean upper torso to left side, while doing chassé right, partners should lean upper torso to right side.

POLKA BASIC

Begin in closed position.

COUNT AND.
Allen hop right, Lisa hop left.

COUNT 1.
Allen step left, Lisa step right.

COUNT AND.
Allen right together left, Lisa left together right.

COUNT 2.
Allen side left, Lisa side right.

This completes first half of basic.

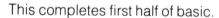

COUNT AND.
Allen hop left, Lisa hop right.

COUNT 1.
Allen side right, Lisa side left.

COUNT AND.
Allen left together right, Lisa right together left.

COUNT 2.
Allen side right, Lisa side left.

If desired, the hop may be omitted. Steps then would start on count 1.

This completes second half of basic. (The basic may be done in left or right turn. While turning basic, dancers' chassés may be done on forward and back diagonals rather than side.)

LEFT OPEN CHASSÉ

Begin by completing full basic—counts and-1-and-2, and-1-and-2, then:

COUNT AND.
Allen hops on right foot, turning into left open (conversation) position, Lisa hop left into open position.

COUNT 1.
Allen forward left, Lisa forward right.

COUNT AND.
Allen forward right, Lisa forward left.

COUNT 2.
Allen forward left, Lisa forward right. NOTE: These steps were done in forward chassé fashion, "chasing" feet rather than passing.

LEFT OPEN CHASSÉ

COUNT AND.
Allen hop left, Lisa hop right.

COUNT 1.
Allen forward right, Lisa forward left.

COUNT AND.
Allen forward left, Lisa forward right.

COUNT 2.
Allen forward right, leading Lisa with his right hand to step in front of him, Lisa forward left, pivoting on her left foot into closed position.

Left open chassé ends in closed position (as illustrated) and may be repeated as many times as desired before ending in such.

Dancers may interpret the lively feeling of the polka by stamping on count 1 or on any and all steps in chassé pattern.

RIGHT OPEN CHASSÉ

Begin with first half of basic, with man releasing right hand from partner's back (on count 2 of first half of basic), then:

COUNT AND.
Allen forward left, Lisa forward right.

COUNT 2.
Allen forward right, Lisa forward left. NOTE: Counts 1-and-2 are done in forward chassé fashion.

COUNT AND.
Allen hops on left foot into right parallel position, Lisa hops on right foot—dancers' arms extending for styling.

COUNT 1.
Allen forward right, Lisa forward left.

COUNT AND.
Allen hop right, Lisa hop left, partners beginning to turn to face each other on hop.

COUNT 1.
Allen forward left, Lisa forward right, Allen's right hand touching Lisa's left hand, palm-to-palm.

COUNT AND.
Allen right together left, Lisa left together right.

COUNT 2.
Allen left together right, Lisa right together left.

COUNT AND.
Allen hops on left foot, Lisa hops on right, Allen's right hand pushing against Lisa's left hand to open once more to right parallel position.

COUNTS 1-AND-2.
This photo shows right parallel position resumed to complete rhythm 1-and-2 (forward chassé fashion). This combination may be repeated as many times as desired.

NOTE: To finish step: When turning into closed position, Allen places arm around Lisa's waist, hand on back—rather than palm-to-palm as previously illustrated. Partners then go into last half of basic.

CHAPTER 5

Fox Trot

With so many dances owing their origins to Europe, Latin America and the Caribbean, it is refreshing to talk about a home-grown American dance that has endured as a modern ballroom classic. Introduced around 1914, the fox trot is credited to Harry Fox, a star of the Ziegfield Follies, who performed what literally was a trotting step to the then popular ragtime rhythm.

The fox trot emphasizes body projection—particularly movement of the rib cage. In this chapter, we will provide instruction in three basic rhythms: *Rhythm A,* slow-quick-quick; *Rhythm B,* slow-slow-quick-quick; and *Rhythm C,* slow-slow-slow-quick-quick. These three basic rhythms all end with two quick steps which usually are done side together. Slow steps usually are done forward or back.

BASIC BOX STEP (Based on Rhythm A)

Begin in closed position.

COUNT 1.
Mark forward left, Kim back right.

COUNT 2.
Use for curved follow through, preparing to step on count 3.

COUNT 3.
Mark side right, Kim side left.

COUNT 4.
Mark left together right, Kim right together left.

COUNT 1.
Mark back right, Kim forward left.

COUNT 2.
Use for curved follow through.

COUNT 3.
Mark side left, Kim side right.

COUNT 4.
Mark right together left, Kim left together right.

Box step usually is done in left turn. Basic Rhythm B may be utilized by man taking two slow steps forward (quick-quicks being side together). Basic Rhythm C may be utilized by man taking three slow forward steps (again, with quick-quick steps as side together). Basic rhythms A-B-C usually are done one set forward and one set back, as illustrated in the basic box step just described. However, basics also may be used to travel in one direction without reversing.

LEFT OPEN CONVERSATION STEP (Based on Rhythm B)

This step, with a slow-slow-quick-quick rhythm, begins in closed position. Man then leads partner into left open position.

COUNT 1.
Mark forward left, Kim forward right.

COUNT 2.
Utilize this count for forward follow through, passing thighs, knees and ankles, preparing to change weight on count 3.

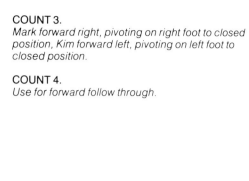

COUNT 3.
Mark forward right, pivoting on right foot to closed position, Kim forward left, pivoting on left foot to closed position.

COUNT 4.
Use for forward follow through.

COUNT 5.
Mark side left, Kim side right.

COUNT 6.
Mark right together left, Kim left together right.

LEFT OPEN TWINKLE (Based on Rhythm A)

Begin this step, which uses a slow-quick-quick rhythm, in closed position.

COUNT 1.
Mark forward left, Kim back right.

COUNT 2.
Curved follow through.

COUNT 3.
Mark side right, pivoting on right foot into left open position, Kim side left, pivoting on left.

COUNT 4.
Mark left together right, Kim right together left.

COUNT 1.
Mark forward right, pivoting on right into closed position, Kim forward left, pivoting on left.

COUNT 2.
Forward follow through.

COUNT 3.
Mark side left, Kim side right.

COUNT 4.
Mark right together left, Kim left together right.

Chapter 6

Rumba

Soft and romantic, the rumba is a flowing dance that quickly becomes a favorite of beginners. Although the music has a definite Latin beat, it also is very melodic, frequently featuring lots of background strings.

The rumba, which was developed in the Caribbean with origins tracing back to Africa, was introduced into the United States from Cuba during the late 1920s. It quickly gained popularity among ballroom dancers, with movie stars George Raft and Carole Lombard among its well-known practitioners.

Footwork in the rumba should be precise. This helps accentuate the Latin look of the dance. The rhythm for the popular medium tempo (one of three tempos, and the one we will teach in this chapter) is quick-quick-slow. The count is 1-2-3-4, with the fourth beat utilizing a curved follow through motion in which the foot does *not* touch the floor (this applies to all count-four steps described in this chapter).

In rumba, steps are taken before weight change occurs, with the hip in a rolling motion. This is part of a movement known as Latin Motion, which it is important to integrate into the dance. Latin Motion is fully described and illustrated in the section following instructions for the rumba basic.

RUMBA BASIC

COUNT 1.
Mark side left, Kim side right. NOTE: For more classical styling, man's lead arm should be higher—just above the small of the back.

COUNT 2.
Mark right together left, Kim left together right.

COUNT 3.
Mark forward left, Kim back right.

COUNT 4.
This count is used for follow through motion, Mark's right foot curving toward his left and off to side, Kim's left foot curving back toward her right and off to side. The change of weight on the side step initiates count 1 of second half of basic, as follows:

COUNT 1.
(Flows from count 4 of first half of basic.)

COUNT 2.
Mark left together right, Kim right together left.

COUNT 3.
Mark back right, Kim forward left.

COUNT 4.
This count is again utilized for curved follow through to side, which would begin basic sequence over.

LATIN MOTION

As a rule of thumb, the leg that is in motion does *not* immediately take the majority of the weight. Most of the weight remains with the hip over the foot that did not move. Work hard on practicing and perfecting Latin Motion, because it is an integral part of Latin dancing, rumba in particular. It absorbs bouncy movements and gives the dancer a smooth motion. And, of course, it adds panache. Keep in mind that Latin Motion involves not only the hips but also motion of the rib cage in opposition to the hips. The hips, rather than just moving side-to-side, gyrate in a forward figure 8. The following sequence of pictures shows Latin Motion during the rumba basic.

COUNT 1.
Mark left foot side left, rib cage to left side, hip over right foot.

COUNT 2.
Mark right together left, rib cage pulling right, hip over left foot. Note earlier comment about footwork being precise—Mark's together should be **together!**

COUNT 3.
Mark forward left, rib cage to left side, hip over right foot.

COUNT 4.
On fourth beat hip begins forward rotation to other side, reaching its destination on count 1.

COUNT 1.
Begin last half of basic.

Latin motion is used in all rumba steps regardless of direction of movement of feet. Rib cage action usually is done by advanced dancers and not beginners.

UNDERARM TURN

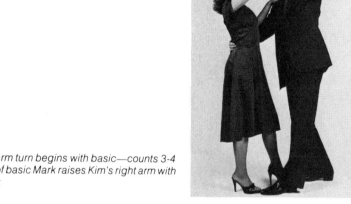

Kim circles to her right on counts 1-2-3, as if to walk around the edge of a small hoop, all forward steps, turn being initiated by body motion rather than turning of feet.

The underarm turn begins with basic—counts 3-4 of last half of basic Mark raises Kim's right arm with his left arm:

COUNT 1.
Mark wraps left foot behind and around right, beginning quarter turn to left while pushing Kim's back with his right hand, guiding her under his arm. Kim steps forward right under arm.

COUNT 2.
Mark steps side right (thus, unwinding wrap), Kim forward left.

COUNT 3.
Mark forward left, taking partner in closed position, Kim forward right.

COUNT 4.
Curved follow through into last half of basic.

CUBAN WALK

Cuban Walk begins at count 3-4 of last half of basic. Mark brings Kim's right arm down with his left arm inward motion, approximately belt high.

COUNT 1.
*Mark crosses left foot behind right. (NOTE: This is **not** a wrap, Mark faces same direction at this point), pushing on Kim's back with his right hand and moving his left arm in a backward motion (the look of a matador taking his cape off to the left— Kim plays the role of the cape!). Kim forward right.*

COUNT 2
Mark side right, Kim forward left (both continue "bullfighter look"), Mark's right hand beginning to move up for style at end of count 2.

COUNT 3.
Mark left together right, pulling his left arm forward, causing Kim to pivot left on left foot. Kim right together left. partners now in parallel position. Note Kim's left arm now styling out and up.

COUNT 4.
Hold with feet together.

Both partners do last half of basic.

COUNT 1.
Mark begins walking with left foot in circle, right shoulder back. Kim forward right in circle, left shoulder forward.

COUNT 2.
Mark back right, Kim forward left.

COUNT 3.
Mark back left, Kim forward right, both still circling and remaining in parallel position.

COUNT 4.
In motion utilizes follow through, back for Mark, forward for Kim.

For next 8 counts Mark is travelling straight back, no turn.

COUNT 1.
Mark back right, Kim forward left. Mark is beginning to lead Kim with left hand to bring her in front of him, partners to finish facing each other at count 3.

COUNT 2.
Mark back left, Kim forward right.

COUNT 3.
Mark back right, Kim forward left.

COUNT 4.
Mark begins back with left foot, Kim begins forward with right foot, Change of weight takes place on count 1, below. NOTE: On these three walking steps Mark is bringing Kim to him in closed position.

COUNT 1.
Mark's arm begins to come down to take Kim.

COUNT 2.
Mark back right, Kim forward left, beginning to secure closed position.

COUNT 3.
Mark back left, Kim forward right. Partners now have resumed closed position.

COUNT 4.
This count initiates follow through into last half of basic.

Then, partners do last half of basic.

CHAPTER 7

Cha-Cha

Cha-cha. The very name of this dance, another import from Cuba, almost urges the feet to pick up the rhythm. Derived from triple-time mambo, the cha-cha is one of the easiest and most fun dances to do. It enjoyed a great surge of popularity in the mid-1950s and continues as a perennial favorite. The story, perhaps apocryphal, of how this dance received its curious name, ascribes "cha-cha" to the sound produced by the heel-less slippers of Caribbean islanders.

Latin Motion, described in the preceding chapter on rumba, should be used, and you will note that in-place steps are used frequently in this dance. Cha-cha is done in a rhythm of quick, quick, quick and split, to a dance count of 1-2-3-and-4. (Up-tempo cha-cha rhythms use less body movement—for example, less driving of the hips.)

CHA-CHA BASIC

Begin in closed position, feet together.

COUNT 1.
Mark forward left, Lisa back right.

COUNT 2.
Mark in place right, Lisa in place left.

COUNT 3.
Mark back left, Lisa forward right.

COUNT AND.
Mark slightly back left, Lisa slightly forward right.

COUNT 4.
Mark back left, Lisa forward right.

This completes first half of basic.

Second half of basic is exact reverse of first, as:

COUNT 1.
Mark back right, Lisa forward left.

COUNT 2.
Mark in place left, Lisa in place right.

COUNT 3.
Mark forward right, Lisa back left.

COUNT AND.
Mark forward left (do not pass other foot), Lisa back right (do not pass other foot.)

COUNT 4.
Mark forward right, Lisa back left (again, counts 3-and-4 are done in chassé fashion).

CHA-CHA CROSSOVER

Count 1-2-3-and-4 utilize first half of basic (page 58).

COUNT 1.
Mark back right, Lisa forward left (as to begin second half of basic).

COUNT 2.
Mark in place left, Lisa in place right. At very end of this count, Mark begins to release right hand from Lisa's back, turning approximately a quarter turn to his right into right parallel position, where count 3 will be executed. Lisa begins a quarter turn to her left to execute count 3.

COUNT 3.
Mark forward right, Lisa forward left.

COUNT AND.
Mark forward left, Lisa forward right.

COUNT 4.
Mark forward right, Lisa forward left. Counts 3-and-4 are done in chassé fashion.

COUNT 1.
Mark forward left, Lisa forward right. Note extension of arms for style.

COUNT 2.
Mark in place right, Lisa in place left.

COUNT 3.
Mark side right, beginning to turn to face partner, Lisa side left, beginning to turn back to partner.

COUNT AND.
Mark right together left, Lisa left together right. NOTE: At this point, partners holding both hands.

COUNT 4.
Mark continues turning body to left, stepping forward left in left parallel position. Lisa continues turning body right, stepping forward right.

Process now to be reversed, as:

COUNT 1.
Mark forward right, Lisa forward left.

Continue reversing for counts 2-3-and-4.

OPEN TURN

This is used to come out of the crossover and many other steps.

COUNT 1.
Mark forward right, Lisa forward left (refer last illustration in crossover sequence, above).

BETWEEN COUNTS
At end of count 1, partners begin rolling off each others arms, Mark turning left while pivoting on right foot half pivot to face opposite direction where count 2 will be executed. Lisa turning to her right, pivoting on left foot half pivot ready to execute count 2. Partners in apart position (no contact).

COUNT 2.
Mark forward left, Lisa forward right, Mark's left hand taking Lisa's right hand.

COUNT 3.
Mark continuing turn, pivoting quarter turn on left foot, taking partner in closed position, stepping right together left. Lisa pivoting on right foot quarter turn, stepping left together right.

COUNT AND.
Mark in place left together right, Lisa in place right together left.

COUNT 4.
Mark in place right together left, Lisa in place left together right.

Open turn may end in closed position (as illustrated) or may end in apart position by man stepping slightly away from partner on count 2 of open forward turn, thereby ending chassé rhythm 3-and-4 facing each other but apart.

HALF CHASE

Half chase begins from apart position, as per immediately preceding description.

COUNT 1.
Mark forward left, Lisa back right, Mark pivoting on left foot half turn to right (right shoulder back) as in following illustration.

COUNT 2.
Mark forward right, Lisa in place left.

COUNT 3.
Mark forward left, Lisa forward right.

COUNT AND.
Mark forward right, Lisa forward left.

COUNT 4.
*Mark forward left, Lisa forward right.
(Count 3-and-4 in forward chassé fashion.)*

COUNT 1.
Mark forward right, Lisa forward left. At end of count 1, Mark pivoting half turn on right foot to left (left shoulder back), Lisa pivoting half turn on left foot to right (right shoulder back).

COUNT 2.
Mark forward left, Lisa forward right.

COUNT 3.
Mark forward right, Lisa forward left.

COUNT AND.
Mark forward left, Lisa forward right. NOTE: moving foot does not pass supporting foot.

COUNT 4.
Mark forward right, Lisa forward left. (Counts 3-and-4 again being done in chassé fashion.)

To end, Mark goes into basic without pivot while facing Lisa.

Mark goes into first half of basic. Lisa does last 4 counts of Mark's steps forward right, pivoting on right with left shoulder back ½ turn—count 1. Forward left count 2 facing Mark. Forward right count 3. Forward left count and. Forward right count 4 (3-and-4 done in chassé fashion).

When Lisa turns to find Mark facing her (visual lead) both she and Mark begin last half of basic on following count 1. (A few basics may be done in apart position.) Mark returns to closed position during chassé portion (counts 3-and-4) of last half of basic by taking slightly larger steps.

CHAPTER 8

Merengue

As with the cha-cha, the merengue originated in the Caribbean, came into popularity in the United States in the 1950s, and is claimed to have an equally colorful genesis. It incorporates a "limp" step that is said to trace back to a general in the Dominican Republic whose guests thought it prudent to imitate his hobbled moves on the dance floor.

Merengue music is similar to a samba rhythm, but is less smooth, is not as melodic, and has a more driving beat. It probably is the easiest of the ballroom dances to learn. Its basic rhythm is 1-2-3-4.

MERENGUE BASIC

COUNT 1.
Mark side left, Lisa side right.

COUNT 2.
Mark right together left, Lisa left together right.

COUNT 3.

Mark side left, Lisa side right. On count 3, Mark's hip moves to right, rib cage to left; exact opposite for Lisa. This movement is common to most third counts in this dance and creates the illusion of a "limp" (however, leg is not locked and does have freedom to move). Beginning dancers may substitute a slight tilt to the side to simulate the rib-cage/hip movement described above.

COUNT 4.

Mark right together left, Lisa left together right.

LEFT OPEN MERENGUE

Begin in closed position.

COUNT 1.

Mark leads Lisa into left open position, stepping forward left, Lisa forward right. Other leg may remain on floor or kick up (as shown) for a more flamboyant look as dancers drop into count 1.

COUNT 2.

Mark forward right, pivoting on right to closed position, Lisa forward left, pivoting on left to closed position.

COUNT 3.

Mark side left, Lisa side right.

COUNT 4.

Mark right together left, Lisa left together right.

MERENGUE SWING

Begin in closed position.

COUNT 1.
Mark back left, releasing hand from Lisa's back, arm moving in an upward motion (which helps to lead Lisa's arm upward). Lisa back right.

COUNT 2.
Mark in place right, bring palm of right hand to Lisa's left. Lisa in place left.

COUNT 3.
Mark side left, Lisa side right. Partners utilize hip and rib-cage movement or, more simply, a slight tilt as shown.

COUNT 4.
Mark in place right, Lisa in place left. Partners begin to push palms away from each other to repeat step as many times as desired. Right turn may be used while working in and away from partner.

Step ends with Mark putting arm around Lisa's waist in place of palm-to-palm.

CIRCLE STEPS

Forward circle steps may be executed by man traveling forward on all steps in circle to left, his partner traveling back. Circle may be wide or tight, depending upon amount of turn initiated.

Back circle steps may be achieved by man taking all back steps, woman taking all forward steps, in circle to right.

Merengue forward motion is achieved by man traveling in a straight line forward, his partner straight back. Merengue back motion would be the reverse. Remember: Count 3 movement should be applied throughout dance.

CHAPTER 9

Tango

Unquestionably, the tango is a dancer's dance, incorporating sophisticated movement and styling and a well-developed sense of knees-bent balance. It is a dance that puts a premium on control; one in which the partners truly move as one. To a ballroom purist, a well-executed tango is as satisfying as is a fluid swing to a golfer.

The tango arrived in the United States and Europe in the early 20th century via the Caribbean and Argentina, where it had the reputation of an erotic dance performed in seedy clubs and dance halls. It quickly caught on in Europe, where exponents of its sensuous dips and bends displayed their expertise at "tango teas," and in the United States where Rudolph Valentino helped to popularize it.

The first three steps in tango dealt with in this chapter will have a rhythm of slow-slow, counts 1-2-3-4. We also will describe a tango close with a rhythm of quick-quick-slow, counts 5-6-7-8. Basic-through-intermediate dancers often tag a tango close on to most steps, as slow-slow-quick-quick-slow, counts 1-2-3-4-5-6-7-8. Tango basic styling features bent knees and all forward motions driving from the hip—which initiates long steps. (Dancers should strive to keep hips over knees so as not to have legs extended too far in front of body.) The dance is best done with close body contact. Tango's characteristic contra-body movement also should be noted.

TANGO BASIC FORWARD MOTION

COUNT 1.
Mark forward left, Kim back right. Mark's upper torso moving left shoulder back, Kim's upper torso moving right shoulder forward (in opposition to feet).

COUNT 2.
(A follow through motion.) Mark's right foot in motion forward, Kim's left foot in motion back, preparing to step on count 3. During follow through, upper torso beginning to reverse position.

COUNT 3.
Mark forward right, Kim back left, Mark's upper torso turning right shoulder back, Kim's upper torso turning left shoulder forward.

COUNT 4.
Mark balance left together right, Kim balance right together left, bodies squared off in closed position. NOTE: This step ended in a balance position, Mark's left foot free ready for next step, Kim's right foot free ready for next step.

TANGO BASIC LEFT OPEN

Begin in closed position, feet together (one foot could be in balance position, such as at end of basic forward motion just described. Mark leads Kim into left open position, then:

COUNT 1.
Mark forward left, Kim forward right. NOTE: Although dancers are stepping into left open position, in the tango this is, by and large, a closed left open position, i.e., shoulders do not open as they did, for example, in the waltz and fox trot; rather, they are more turned in to each other.

COUNT 2.
Forward follow through. During count 2, Mark is leading Kim with right hand on back, as to cause her to take next step, count 3, in front of him.

COUNT 3.
Mark forward right, Kim forward left approxmately 2-6 inches in front of Mark's right foot. Mark continuing to lead Kim with his right hand, causing Kim to pivot on her left into closed position. Actual pivot would occur on count 4.

COUNT 4.
Pivot (above). NOTE: Mark ending left foot in balance together right, Kim right foot in balance together left, as in end of Tango Basic Forward Motion.

BASIC CORTE (Dip)

Let's again note that partners stand in close contact, knees bent and hips over knees—a position that would be awkward to simply stand in, but one which, when incorporated into this dance movement, produces cat-like motion. Begin basic corte in closed position, feet together. However, if moving into this step from another, partners would be in balance positions, as previously noted. Neither partner will tilt from the waist up in any direction during this step.

COUNT 1.
Mark back left, Kim forward right. NOTE: Partners do not bend knees beyond the point prescribed for closed position. In taking his step, Mark steps directly back, hips staying squared off, being careful not to turn body. Kim steps directly forward being sure not to turn body. Kim has total control of her weight throughout this step.

COUNT 2.
Mark's body continues to move back over supporting leg (his left), Kim continues to move forward over her supporting leg (her right). During this count Kim's left foot turning in on ball of foot (turn out), left heel elevated and moving forward. Mark keeps right foot flat on floor.

COUNT 3.
Mark pushes forward with upper part of body (initiating movement from hips), transferring weight to right foot, Mark's left heel raising and turning into body (turn out). Kim's weight, therefore, will shift to her left foot, her left heel dropping to the floor.

COUNT 4.
Mark balance left together right, Kim balance right together left, closed position.

TANGO FAN

Begin in closed position. Rhythm of this step is quick-quick-slow-slow-slow-slow—or any even number of slow steps.

COUNT 1.
Mark forward left, Kim back right.

COUNT 2.
Mark begins to move Kim to his right side (right side position). Mark in place right, Kim forward diagonal left.

COUNT 3.
Mark places left foot to side, heel of left foot off floor, all weight over right foot, leading Kim with right hand past his right side, Kim forward right.

COUNT 4.
Mark's feet remain in place. Mark leads Kim with his right hand into left open position, Kim pivoting on right foot into left open position. Kim's left foot fanning floor using inside of ball of left foot (as if to describe an arc on the floor). NOTE: Kim's supporting leg (her right) remains bent so as to avoid up-down movement. Fan leg in flex.

COUNT 5.
Mark continues to lead Kim forward as his position remains constant, causing Kim to step forward left. As Kim's weight goes to left foot, Mark already is beginning to turn her into right side position, causing fan to begin, Kim pivoting on left, her right foot fanning (describing an arc).

COUNT 6.
Kim finishes fan with right foot behind left, still on inside of ball of foot in right side position.

COUNT 5.
To end fan sequence, repeat counts 3-4-5, Mark leading Kim to step in front of him, Kim stepping forward left foot 2-6 inches in front of Mark's right.

COUNT 6.
Mark leads Kim into closed position as he draws his left foot in balance position together right. Kim, pivoting on left foot, ending right foot in balance together left. NOTE: Kim's ending same as tango basic left open.

Fanning procedure may be repeated as many times as desired, using first 3-4-5-6 counts.

TANGO CLOSE

The tango close, usually done to a rhythm of quick-quick-slow, is an element of dance that usually is tacked on to most tango steps by beginning-through-intermediate dancers. As you become more knowledgeable about and proficient in this dance you probably will find yourself making less use of the tango close—except, perhaps, at the end of a phrase of music. Begin in closed position—usually at a balance, as previously described, then:

COUNT 1.
Mark forward left, Kim back right. Mark's left side of upper torso turns back, Kim's right side of upper torso turns forward.

COUNT 2.
Mark side right, upper torso tilting slightly to left, Kim side left, upper torso tilting to right.

COUNT 3.
Mark's left foot begins to slide toward right on ball of left foot, Kim's right foot begins to slide toward her left on ball of right foot. Bodies are beginning to straighten.

COUNT 4.
Mark's left foot reaches together right, still on ball of left foot in balance position, Kim's right foot reaches together left, still on ball of right foot in balance position. NOTE: Dancers' feet continue to move during counts 3-4. At this point, bodies are level in closed position. In phrasing to music more advanced dancers may use any number of counts to close.

When dancers add tango close to tango basic forward motion, they do *not* come to a balance at the end of basic. Rather, they continue count 4 in motion to step on count 1 of tango close.

When tango close is added to left open tango basic, dancers *do* come to balance at count 4; then they step out for count 1 of tango close.

To add tango close to basic corte, do *not* come to balance. Instead, leg continues to move into count 1 of tango close as is done in tango basic forward motion.

Dancers may make a combination of the first three basic tango steps described in this chapter by doing: tango basic forward motion into left open tango basic into basic corte (dip), coming out of corte with tango close.

CHAPTER 10

Mambo

In the late 1940s, mambo came out of the cane fields of Cuba and into the clubs of Havana and the ballrooms of London, New York and other cities in Europe and the United States. By the 1950s, band leader Pérez Prado had become the dance's most famous advocate, helping to popularize mambo the way Xavier Cougat had the rumba.

Mambo, a lively marriage of Latin American and jazz rhythms, affords lots of opportunity for freestyle dancing as partners move from closed to open positions. It is done to single-, double- and triple-time rhythm, with single-time being the most popular. However, good dancers are able to move freely from single- to double-time. The steps detailed in this chapter utilize single-time rhythm. The basic mambo steps off on count 2, counts being 2-3-4-1 (quick-quick-slow), with count 1 being used for follow through.

MAMBO BASIC

Partners begin in closed position, feet together.

COUNT 1.
Hold.

COUNT 2.
Mark forward left, Kim back right.

COUNT 3.
Mark in place right, Kim in place left.

COUNT 4.
Mark back left, Kim forward right. NOTE: This completes first half of basic. Direction in which these steps are taken is exactly the same as in the cha-cha basic—but without chassé rhythm. Second half of basic is done simply by reversing first half (remember count 1 used for follow through!) and beginning with the other foot, man's right, woman's left.

CROSSOVER

Do first half of basic, 2-3-4, next count 1 used for follow through, Mark's right leg swinging back, Kim's left leg swinging forward, then:

COUNT 2.
Mark back right, Kim forward left.

COUNT 3.
Mark in place left, Kim in place right. At the ends of counts 3 through 4 Mark releases right arm from Kim's back, turning into right parallel position. NOTE: Slight pivot may occur on Mark's left and Kim's right during change of position, preparing for count 4.

COUNT 4.
Mark forward right, Kim forward left in parallel position (arms beginning to move out and up for style).

COUNT 1.
Forward follow through, Mark left foot, Kim right foot.

COUNT 2.
Mark forward left, Kim forward right, remaining in right parallel position.

COUNT 3.
Mark in place right, Kim in place left, starting to turn Mark pivoting on right foot left shoulder back, Kim pivoting on left foot right shoulder back (as to go through closed position into left parallel position). NOTE: In steps such as crossover, going from right to left or left to right parallel do not release one hand of partner until you have the other.

COUNT 4.
Mark forward left, Kim forward right in left parallel position.

Continue crossover by reversing and repeating as many times as desired counts 2-3-4 of right open segment of chase. Dancers would end mambo crossover the same as they ended cha-cha crossover, with open forward turn (except that mambo uses counts 2-3-4 rather than 1-2-3-and-4).

KICK STEP

Partners dance into right parallel position, as in crossover. (Rhythm of kick step is 2-3-4-1-and-2-and-3-4).

COUNT 1.
Mark's left foot in forward motion right parallel position, Kim's right foot in forward motion.

COUNT 2.
Mark forward left, Kim forward right.

COUNT 3.
Mark in place right, Kim in place left, beginning to turn to closed position.

COUNT 4.
Mark side left, Kim side right, partners holding both hands.

COUNT 1.
(In this case, count 1 is used as an integral part of the step, rather than just as follow through.) Mark kicks right, crossing in front of left, Kim kicks left leg, crossing in front of right. NOTE: Kick step usually is done from knee down, not from hip, with foot arched and low to the floor. Also note that Mark's right arm is leading Kim's left arm slightly down and toward center, his left arm raising Kim's right arm slightly. This movement helps to lead Kim into kick.

COUNT AND.
Mark in place right, Kim in place left.

COUNT 2.
Mark tapping ball of left foot together right, left knee isolation in, Kim tapping ball of right foot together left, right knee isolation in. Note the arm movement that helps prevent partners from changing weight on tap segment: Mark's left hand leading Kim's right hand toward center, Mark's right hand taking Kim's left hand slightly up and in to body.

COUNT AND 3.
Mark in place left, Kim in place right, ball of Mark's right foot together left, right knee isolation in, ball of Kim's left foot together right, left knee isolation in. Mark's right arm leads Kim's left arm in toward center of body. Mark's left arm leads Kim's right arm slightly up and into body.

COUNT 4.
Mark's right hand releases Kim's left, moving into right parallel position. Mark forward right, Kim forward left.

You now are in position to repeat kick step as many times as desired. End kick step with open forward turn, ending in closed or apart position. If ending in apart position, you may do a half chase, as in cha-cha (using, of course, mambo rather than cha-cha rhythm).

CHAPTER 11

Samba

In Brazil, where this dance originated, the Samba has virtually become the national dance. It is a happy dance, less exacting than other Latin American exports. Basic styling has dancers leaning back on forward steps and forward on back steps. Dancers also lean the upper torso to the left when stepping side right and lean the upper torso to the right when stepping side left. This forward, back and side motion of the body produces a distinctive barrel-roll effect.

Tracing its roots back to African slaves, the samba travelled from Rio de Janeiro to New York to debut at the 1939 World's Fair and was popularized in movies that featured Carmen Miranda (of the tongue-rolling accent and elaborate fruit-laden headwear). Following World War II, the dance was a favorite in Europe and the United States.

Samba uses a chassé rhythm (quick-and-split-1-and-2), counts 1-and-2-3-and-4.

SAMBA BASIC

Begin in closed position, feet together.

COUNT 1.
Mark forward left, Lisa back right.

COUNT AND.
Mark forward right, Lisa back left.

COUNT 2.
Mark left together right, Lisa right together left.

This concludes first half of basic.

COUNT 3.
Mark back right, Lisa forward left.

COUNT AND.
Mark back left, Lisa forward right.

COUNT 4.
Mark right together left, Lisa left together right.

Basic usually is done turning left, although it may be executed without turns.

This concludes basic.

LEFT OPEN CHASSÉ

Partners complete full basic, then Mark leads Lisa into left open position. (In a "close" closed position, lead is enhanced by man raising his right elbow which, in turn, raises the woman's left elbow as well as turning hand on back.

COUNT 1.
Mark forward left, Lisa forward right.

COUNT AND.
Mark forward right, Lisa forward left, as in chassé fashion (do not pass foot).

COUNT 2.
Mark pulls left foot back, crossing in front of right on ball of left foot. Lisa pulls right foot back, crossing in front of left on ball of right foot. Dancers may be on balls of both feet in this position.

COUNT 3.
Mark forward right, Lisa forward left.

COUNT AND.

Mark forward left, Lisa forward right, as in chassé fashion (do not pass foot).

COUNT 4.

Mark pulls right foot back, crossing in front of left, Lisa pulls left foot back, crossing in front of right, once more on balls of front feet or both feet. NOTE: 1-&-and counts are done in relaxed but upright position (no lean); on pulling counts 2 and/or 4, body leans forward.

Left open chassé may be repeated as many times as desired. To end this step, Mark would step in place right foot count 4 (replacing count 4 above) instead of crossing, while leading Lisa with hand on back, moving her forward to cause her to step left foot in front of him (rather than her cross). Mark turns Lisa with hand on back, causing her to pivot on left foot into closed position.

Left open chasse also may be led into from crossover (instructions for crossover follow).

CROSSOVER

Begin in closed position.

COUNT 1.
Mark side right, Lisa side left.

COUNT AND
Mark crosses right back of left on ball of foot, Lisa crosses left back of right on ball of foot.

COUNT 2.
Mark in place left, Lisa in place right.

This completes first half of crossover. Last half is accomplished by reversing procedure, opposite feet doing side, cross, in place. The crossover may be repeated as many times as desired.

RIGHT OPEN CHASSÉ

COUNT 1.
Mark leads Lisa into right parallel position, forward right, Lisa forward left.

COUNT AND.
Mark forward left, Lisa forward right (chassé fashion).

COUNT 2.
Mark right foot pulling back crossing in front of left on ball of foot, Lisa left foot pulling back crossing in front of right. Style as in left open chassé.

COUNT 3.
Mark forward left, crossing left in front of right, beginning movement into closed position. Lisa forward right, crossing right in front of left, beginning to return to closed position.

Right open chassé may be led into after first half of basic or first half of crossover.

COUNT AND.
Mark forward right, Lisa forward left (chassé fashion). NOTE: At end of this count, Mark's right palm approaching Lisa's left palm.

COUNT 4.
Mark left foot pulling back crossing in front of right, Lisa right foot back crossing in front of left. At this point, Mark is pushing right palm against Lisa's left palm, preparing to open once more into right parallel position to repeat step as many times as desired.

To end step, instead of crossing on count 4, Mark would step forward in front of Lisa, pivoting on left foot to closed position, Lisa in place right. Then, while turning left (left shoulders back), partners would go into last half of basic.

INDEX